STARSEEDS FOR BEGINNERS

Everything you Need to Know about Starseed Types,How to Know if you are a Starseed and What Starseed are you

Ramon Tibbs
Copyright@2022

TABLE OF CONTENT

CHAPTER 1

INTRODUCTION

If you have ever looked up at the night sky and felt a connection with a dazzling cluster of stars or a brilliant planet, you may be sensing your soul's connection to a previous or future existence. It's possible that you can feel this connection all the way down to your bones, given that you sprang from stardust and have been imbued with divine light. Is my mind playing tricks on me? Or did you originate from a faraway star, becoming a direct ancestor of a light body or planet that was located in the void of space?

It took hundreds of years of research, and more recently, more exact evaluations, but scientists currently believe that there are over ten billion galaxies in the universe that is known to us. There are estimates that the Milky Way, which is the galaxy in which we reside, has more than 100 billion individual stars.

That number refers to the number of stars that can be seen in the observable universe. Despite the fact that this is an enormous number, just think of the billions of kingdoms and planets that are concealed from plain sight. Imagine the additional miles that we still have to cover. Think about the notion that time is an illusion and that everything in the universe either evolves or extends with each passing instant. Could it be that the number of realms, galaxies, planets, and stars is always changing, and as a result, it is impossible to estimate? If this is the case, then your birth on Earth was either something you predetermined to happen or something that happened by chance.

When we think about where we came from, we can explore the possibility that the Earth was one of many experiments conducted during a time when several extraterrestrial cultures worked together to seed stars and planets in order to build new worlds. It would appear that we are presented with a number of choices once we pass away and decide whether or not to be reincarnated. Because we are souls that wander through space and time, we must take into account not just this planet but also the countless other worlds, realms, and universes that exist across the multiverse, as well as the numerous spacetime continuums. Our souls may have been reborn this manner a thousand times in a thousand other universes. This is one possible explanation. It's also possible that we're leading parallel lives that are intertwined in a number of different locations and over a number of different spacetime platforms.

The Earth is a constantly changing, three-dimensional world that maintains a healthy equilibrium between the realms of the physical and the angelic experiences. Because of this, it is possible that millions of Starseed have made the decision to dwell among us in the hopes that they might help or profit from our style of vulnerability, the karmic cycles of rebirth that occur on Earth, and our planet's ongoing expansion.

CHAPTER 2

What Kinds Of Resources Did Humans Use To Learn About Starseeds?

Channelers and seers who maintain frequent connections with the Akashic records are the ones who brought the thoughts and notions around Starseeds to our attention. These records include the energy imprints of all intentions, thoughts, emotions, relationships, creations, and events that have ever taken place across all races, in all realms, and over the entirety of spacetime. These imprints may be found in the records. Although most of this knowledge may be channeled and understood with reasonable ease, there are a variety of points of view regarding the process by which Starseeds arrive on Earth and the many different sorts of Starseeds.

Who or what exactly is a starseed?

The channelers claim that Starseeds are highly evolved spiritual beings that originate from other worlds and dimensions and who are in possession of spiritual and scientific knowledge that dates back hundreds of thousands of years. It would appear that the majority of Starseeds are benevolent creatures with the goal of assisting all living beings throughout all of the realms and universes; but, there are some Starseeds that have the goal of

controlling interplanetary
resources for the benefit of their
home planets.

The majority of people believe
that Starseeds are wandering
souls from other worlds that
incarnated on Earth in order to
uplift and cure humankind as
well as take part in the
progression of the planet. There
is also the possibility that these
Starseeds are the physical
progeny of extraterrestrials from
other worlds who made the
journey to Earth in order to
serve as lightworkers for our
planet.

CHAPTER 3

Types of Starseeds

It would appear that the majority of Starseeds have come to Earth in order to teach and heal the people who live here; nevertheless, not all Starseeds have the intention of assisting humanity's spiritual development. Some of them have traveled to our world for their own advantage, while others are here to help more sinister endeavors. Despite how exotic they may seem, not every soul has objectives that are founded on love and light.

The following is a list of some of the more well-known and widespread types of Starseeds.

11

The planets Sirius A and Sirius B are where these Sirian souls originally hail from. The star Sirius A shines brighter than any other star visible from Earth's surface. It is believed that the ancestors of the people who live on Earth originated from the star Vega, which is located in the Lyra constellation. The Miengu and Merpeople call the lesser star Sirius B, which is located in the constellation Sirius, their home. The awakening of every single human being was kicked off by these two planets. It is stated that Ascended Masters such as Jesus and Mother Mary came to mankind from the Sirius A star system.

$$$

The Pleiades, which may also be referred to as the Seven Sisters,

Messier 45, and The Eye of the Bull, are a star cluster that can be located in the constellation Taurus. These Starseeds originate from the Pleiades. The logo for the Subaru vehicle brand incorporates a stylized version of this cluster. The record keepers for Earth are the Pleiadians, and they assert that the age of the globe is greater than 600 billion years. The Pleiadians inhabit a frequency that corresponds to the fifth dimension, which is the source of both love and creative inspiration. They have a matriarchal culture that places a high value on the well-being of families, children, and women. The Pleiadians have a behavior pattern that is quite similar to that of humans, with the exception that they are far more emotionally and spiritually mature. Although many of them have arrived to Earth to assist in the expansion of awareness and evolution of life here, some of them could utilize their superior abilities to manipulate humans.

These deep individuals hail from the planet Arcturus, which is home to the most technologically sophisticated civilisation in our galaxy. They are creatures from the fifth dimension and they constructed a society that ended up serving as the model for how people should live on Earth. Arcturians are highly evolved on a mental and emotional level, and it was always the intention for them to serve as humanity's spiritual shamans and healers. Some people believe that after a person dies, they go through Arcturian energy architecture on their way from this life to the next life that they will eventually have. Arcturus has the sense of a heavenly world, similar to all cultures that exist on the fifth through the ninth dimensions. However, it can serve as an advantageous landing site for etheric forms, nonphysical consciousness, and rebirthing souls, allowing them to once again grow used to a grounded, physical world. The Bootes constellation contains Arcturus, which is the brightest star in the constellation.

Andromedans are a telepathic, caring, and altruistic people that hail from the spiral-shaped Andromeda Galaxy, also known as MS31 or M31. These magnificent individuals have one goal: to free the races that have been enslaved by the Reptilians and replace their oppression with love and harmony. Not only do Andromedan creatures have a strong emphasis on the heart, but they are also highly evolved mentally and experts in every scientific field. The Andromedan has a singular place in the cosmos due to the harmony that exists between their left and right hemispheres.

Indigo, Crystal, and Rainbow: Individuals that belong to these three soul types frequently have exceptional or supernatural skills, such as telepathy, clairvoyance, light-emanation, energy-cleansing, profound empathy, and reality-shifting. These are only some of the talents they may have. Indigos are imbued with the power of Archangel Michael, and as a result, they have a difficult time tolerating situations that they perceive to be unjust. Crystals are typically more kind and generous than their Indigo and Rainbow siblings because they are imbued with the brightness, joy, and clarity that are associated with the archangel Gabriel. Rainbow children are the most recent group of healing souls to arrive on Earth. These youngsters frequently receive a diagnosis of autism spectrum disorder. These three groups, each of which has a natural detachment from the material world, view contacts with this world not as opportunities to advance personally but rather as spiritual exercises. According to

17

the legend, these lightworkers' soul groups in faraway galaxies urged them to provide their services to mankind on Earth without expecting anything in return.

Lightworker: The Lightworker are exceptional souls from a range of worlds and dimensions who have consented to incarnate on Earth and other worlds in order to assist in the process of spiritual evolution. They always choose lives that advance mankind and enhance the degree of consciousness of those who are in their immediate vicinity. They have as their major mission the promotion of goodness, love, and kindness toward all other sentient beings they come into contact with. Lightworkers are

18

not bound to any one planet, community, culture, or mission in any way. They dedicate their entire lives to serving the light.

Orion: The Orions will investigate everything in great detail and question it. They intend to make an effort to produce living entities here on Earth that are centered on the intellect. They are preoccupied with research and the scientific method, but tragically, they do not have a grasp of their own emotions. The purpose of the Orion mission here on Earth is to assist in enhancing our comprehension of the significance of scientific research. Their individual and collective spiritual aim is to acquire from humanoids the skills necessary to become more trustworthy and loyal. While some Orions aspire to enlightenment, others serve as agents for the Reptilians and other aliens that aim to dominate Earth rather than free it from their tyranny.

These entities from the Lyra constellation may be seen represented in the artwork of Earth's ancient civilizations, most notably Egypt, with its feline-headed gods and goddesses. Felines are associated with the Lyra constellation. These entities have psychic and telepathic abilities, and they have a tendency to cultivate spiritual capabilities rather than skills that feed or help their physical reality. They spend much of their time in higher realms, where they seek connections with the eternal consciousness in order to achieve light, clarity, and abundance in their lives. The Felines bestow elegance onto humans and hope upon all living things on Earth, inspiring creativity in each and every one of them.

$$$

Maldek was a planet in our solar system that had characteristics that were comparable to those of Earth. Its inhabitants got dependent on robotic technologies, quite similar to the way things have progressed here on Earth, and as a result, they finally became ill and indolent. Because of their insatiable desire for power, they annihilated their home planet, which forced some of them to look for a new place to call home here on Earth. The Maldek have gained wisdom from their past errors and now aim to impart that knowledge to humanoids, in the hopes that they would motivate them to make wiser decisions about politics, technology, health, and communication.

Both Lemuria and Atlantis were formerly home to ancient civilizations that made significant contributions to the fields of philosophy, spirituality, and the medical arts before being submerged in Earth's oceans. They are supposed to have been the first Starseed tribes to engage in direct trade with peoples from other worlds. Both the Lemurians and the Atlanteans found success on Earth thanks to their

inventiveness and their
dedication to technological
progress. In the end, like like
Maldek, these nations
annihilated themselves due to
greed, idleness, and sickness.
Despite the fact that these
circumstances were extremely
detrimental, the numerous
ideas, inventions, and spiritual
qualities that were produced
were not destroyed. Some of the
most evolved souls from these
cultures were saved and turned
into Starseed to be planted on
other planets and incarnations
across the universe, including
those that will take place on
Earth in the present and the
future.

Reptilian: These shape-shifters,
who are also known as Lizard
People, Saurians, and
Draconians, want to rule Earth

for their own egotistical gain and are thus called Reptilians. David Icke has published a study on the Reptilians, in which he notes that these beings are want political power on Earth in order to affect human civilizations, cultures, and the progression of humankind. Many people are under the impression that certain Reptilians with changed physical looks are currently residing among us. Some individuals believe that reptilian spirits may infiltrate the bodies of our most prominent leaders and influence them to abandon principles and choices that would be to the advantage of the people living on this planet. Fortunately for the Reptilians, they have a lot of opponents who dwell in the light and have taken it upon themselves to fight against all darkness.

There is also the possibility that starseeds were born as a result of inter-consciousness conception or virgin births, similar to the accounts told about Jesus. There is also the possibility that every soul has the potential to become a Starseed if another Starseed fills the soul with their own deliberate brightness. This is something that may happen to souls while they are still in the womb or at any other time in their existence.

In any case, it would appear that Starseeds do indeed exist, but in a somewhat different form. It's possible that we'll never know which of the

Starseed theories are the most accurate.

CHAPTER 4

How Can One Determine Whether or Not They Are a Starseed?

You could have a nagging feeling that you originated from somewhere other than this planet, and you might be able to picture how your body looked in previous incarnations, on other planets. It's possible that you fantasize about living in other galaxies in the hopes of one day really reincarnating in one of those places. You could be curious in how you arrived here as well as whether or not you would ever go back. Even while you have these actual

26

experiences of harmony with other worlds, it is possible that you may never know for certain whether or not you are a Starseed.

Every one of us longs to feel like we belong, that we are aligned with, or that we are related to another individual, family, community, culture, or society. We want for acceptance and connection in order to have our hearts filled and to be inspired. We decorate ourselves with labels that give us the impression that we are exceptional or one of a kind so that we may better understand where we may fit in. We could say something like, "I'm a seven on the Enneagram," "I'm a recovering Catholic," or "I'm a conservative Democrat." These

27

are all examples of self-descriptions. We could even declare something along the lines of "I am Starseed, Pleiadian, to be more specific."

We have a strong attachment to our transient self-identities, also known as the personality constructions that we use to establish our personas, relationships, and lives, regardless of whether or not they are founded in reality. When conventional labels and stereotypes don't cut it, we go elsewhere—sometimes even to the heavens—for answers.

This does not imply that the reality you have been living as a Starseed is false. The purpose of this is to introduce the concept that our birth, imagined, and

assumed identities may all be
illusory, at the very least in part.

CHAPTER 5

Starseed Personalities and Traits
Characteristics of the Body and
Capabilities

There is a great deal of
discussion over the particular
physical characteristics of
Starseeds. Although there are
many who believe that
Starseeds are tall and slender,
or have large eyes and broad
foreheads, a soul that is
pursuing its growth does not
need to have a certain physical
form in particular. It is accurate
to claim that Starseeds may be

found in a wide variety of forms and dimensions. It is via resonance and alignment that the soul is brought into the bosom of a living creature, and it is this process that allows the soul to take on a bodily form. When it comes to our spiritual development and awakening, the physical characteristics we possess are inconsistent along these lines and have very little significance overall.

$$$

It is possible to say the same thing about the capabilities of Starseeds. Every living thing serves a certain purpose, and that function is what spawns the skills and abilities that are unique to that being's soul. Starseeds do not monopolize any one sector of the economy, and not every one of them possesses the same skills, qualities, or capabilities as the others. Starseeds are exactly like the rest of us in that they can have careers as machinists, teachers, dancers, artists, politicians, or dissatisfied stock analysts. They can also feel melancholy, joyous, wild, constrained, limited, or expansive.

Sensitivity on both the Emotional and Social Levels

It's possible that Starseeds have a higher developed capacity for emotional intelligence and empathy than other people have. It goes to reason that Starseeds could have the kindest hearts and the most acute intuition, given the wide diversity of beliefs and experiences they have most certainly encountered during their lives, as well as the fact that they have lived in a number of different universes. Having said that, every soul is capable of wandering off course, and even a soul that has done so is capable of returning to its original path at any time and with only one consistent choice.

Both Intelligence and Consciousness Can Be Developed

When Starseeds are a part of spiritual lineages that strive to serve mankind, it is possible that they will have greater levels of intellect and a more enlarged collective consciousness than when they are not a part of such lineages. There is a possibility that the sole mission of certain Starseed is to work as healers or spiritual gurus in order to aid humankind. It's possible that others came to Earth in order to clear their karma or get better.

The notion that all Starseeds are more advanced than human beings is a fallacy, despite the fact that it may seem intriguing or romantic to entertain such a notion. Every soul, whether it originates from this planet or another, is working toward achieving its goal. On some level, every soul is interested in gaining information, expanding their experiences, or both. Your birthright is to embrace intelligence, seek an enlarged awareness, and completely

33

awaken at any moment, regardless of whether or not you are a Starseed or are from Jersey.

Feelings That Are Not of This World

Anyone who has launched themselves into a more profound awareness by letting go of their birth narrative and everything else that goes along with it has accomplished this feat. They have allowed themselves to become emotionally and intellectually open, which has liberated them from the most fundamental limitations. A Starseed may have a highly developed soul, and as a result, they are able to comprehend and concord with the characteristics of the nature of other worlds. It would be a wonderful present for you if this were the case.

You may expose yourself to the enlarged collective awareness that permeates all matter and non-matter by doing so regardless of where you came from or who you are. This is because the consciousness is present in everything. Your title, your ethnicity, or your ancestry do not confine you in any way. You are a lot more than you may realize at this moment.

If you wish to explore other planets, you must first beckon them to you. Find ways to fulfill both your hobbies and your curiosities. However, in the end, the things that you are calling may divert your attention away from the expansion that you are looking for.

CHAPTER 6

STARSEED TYPES EXPLAINED INDEPTH

It is useful to understand what I truly mean when I refer to a starseed type before we move on to discussing the many varieties of starseeds.

What are the different kinds of starseeds?

The group of spiritual beings that come from a variety of places in the universe is referred to as "starseed types," and the phrase "starseed types" is used to characterize this group.

They have been dispatched to our world to complete a specific purpose, the primary objective of which is to offer assistance to the people who live here during times of transition. They are able to achieve this by employing the profound knowledge that they have acquired through the events that have occurred in their worlds.

They are drawn to our world because they comprehend the interdependence of all forms of life, which is the reason for their arrival here. They are aware that no entity can exist outside of the whole, and as a result, their goal is to assist those of us living on planet Earth by fostering oneness and working to improve the status of our world.

The human race requires direction as our planet enters a crucially critical transitional phase in order to make certain that they do not make the same mistakes as in the past and to establish a global environment in which all species may flourish.

Your starseed type not only reveals the solar system from whence you originally came, but it also explains why you made the conscious decision to manifest on Earth in the first place.

The list of starseed species is rather large; but, there are some that are more likely to appear on our planet, and others are more likely to incarnate someplace else in the Universe. Some of these races have a higher chance of becoming humans.

How Can I Determine Where My Starseed Soul Came From?

Finding out which starseed type you are shouldn't be too difficult, but it does involve some serious introspection from the one doing the figuring out.

If you want to know for sure which category you fall into, you will need to do a personality test and be completely forthright with yourself about the state of your internal life.

Just by entertaining the possibility that you are a starseed, you have already accomplished a critical milestone on the path to understanding your actual identity.

$$$

The awakening that comes from discovering your starseed type is life-changing. You are suddenly endowed with a sense of clarity, a profound understanding, and a strong need to get out into the world and carry out the work for which you were sent on this planet.

Starseed types are frequently highly adept at concealing

themselves under the mask of form that we refer to as "human beings."

Discovering which starseed type you are is a uniquely personal experience; but, as your awareness grows, you may discover that you are able to distinguish between various types of starseeds.

It's a revelation that, much like learning about numerology, has the potential to have a profound impact on your life.

On the other hand, it is not up to you to determine whether or not other people belong to a certain starseed kind. Their epiphany must arise from their innate curiosities, just as yours did from yours, just as yours did with you.

Certain activities have the potential to stimulate the profound introspection that is necessary to arrive at the conclusion that one is a starseed. Meditation is one of the most successful approaches, and you may see my video on YouTube to learn how to meditate in the most effective way possible.

What Are the Various Types of Starseeds Available?

The following is a list of the 10 most prevalent starseed races

and the primary traits
associated with them:

Seeds of the Orion Nebula

The Orion constellation is home
to a wide array of planets and
stars, all of which contribute to
the formation of Orion
starseeds. They are one of the
varieties of starseeds that
incarnate on Earth more
frequently than any other kind.
The following characteristics are
the most telling that you are of
this starseed type:

You have an innate curiosity
towards things having to do with
science.

You are more prone to thinking
conceptually and rationally
rather than emotionally.

Even when things are difficult, you maintain a positive outlook. This is shown in your sense of humor as well as your inclination to maintain a cheerful attitude regardless of the challenges that life presents to you.

You are self-controlled and have a strong sense of discipline.

You have an entrepreneurial spirit and a strong desire to motivate people by sharing your successes with them.

Starseeds of the Arcturian Race

Arcturian starseeds are regularly incarnated on Earth, and their origin may be traced back to the star Arcturus, which is located in the Bootes constellation. If you are a member of this starseed, the information that follows will probably ring true for you.

You are of the opinion that progress made in technological fields is very significant to the survival of the human species.

You have no fear of death, and the thought of departing from your physical body brings you a sense of calm and acceptance.

You have a natural aptitude for mathematics and take pleasure in resolving issues involving numbers.

Even though you try to keep your emotions under check, you have a lot of sympathy for other people.

When you are overpowered by negative feelings, you frequently lose your cool and get irritated.

45

You have an unusually high sensitivity to stimuli from the outside world, such as bright lights, loud noises, and certain odors.

Pleiadian Starseeds

Pleiadian starseeds are able to incarnate on Earth from different realms because their home star system, the Pleiades, is composed of seven luminous stars. Among their characteristics are:

a tendency toward introversion as well as shyness, particularly around new people.

I get the distinct impression that I should be working on humanitarian issues.

Having a pronounced jawline and cheekbones are examples of

desirable physical characteristics.

possessing a profound awareness of the significance of one's family as well as a great desire to assist one's loved ones.

because of their drive to please other people, they put themselves in situations where they might be exploited.

having the sense that they are here on Earth to complete a task that is of the utmost significance to them.

Sirian Starseeds

The ancient Egyptians were captivated by the star Sirius and the mysteries it held for them. The Sirian starseeds are said to have originated from a binary star system that contains the brightest star that can be seen in the night sky. The following characteristics are indicators that you are a member of the starseed race.

You devote a significant portion of your life to spirituality, yet you also believe in earthly things and pursue worldly goals.

Even when other people make an effort to provoke you, you don't find yourself in an angry condition very often.

You would rather have a select few people who can truly be called friends than a vast number of people who are just passing through your life.

You give the impression of being closed off to your love partners and are, in fact, closed off in your relationships.

It's clear that canines hold a particular place in your heart.

Starseeds of the Draconians

The Draconian starseed variety has an inextricable connection to dragons and other reptiles. They are native to the constellation Draco and possess a number of traits that set them apart, including the following:

Having a profound aversion to being ruled and having power thrust upon one.

Making certain that they are successful in completing whatever work, task, or project that they take on. Draconian starseeds abhor the feeling of having anything incomplete in their lives.

Having a body temperature that is significantly lower than usual and having a strong affinity for warmer locations.

If they are not in alignment, they have a tendency to become too driven by money when they make decisions.

$$$

Lyran Starseeds

Those who are of the Lyran starseed race hail from the Lyra constellation, which contains a few stars that were birthed on the Vega planet. These people came to Earth from the Lyra constellation. It is believed that the earliest human beings originated in Lyra, and if you possess any of the characteristics listed below, it is possible that you, too, originated there.

You are not one to shy away from labor that is strenuous and physically demanding. You enjoy it!

It appears that your needs for sleep are greater than those of the normal individual.

You are a well-balanced person, yet when the opportunity presents itself, you enjoy going all in and taking a chance on something.

You have a propensity to begin new endeavors with zeal and passion, but when you become bored, you find it difficult to see them through to completion.

The pursuit of pleasure through travel is really necessary.

Some of your features, such as your eyes, could have a feline or bird-like quality to them, such as a pointed snout or eyes that are slightly tilted up.

Starseeds from the planet Mars

Some people think that Martians came to Earth many hundreds of thousands of years ago in order to assist humans in the process of their own evolutionary development. We know the following about this starseed kind, despite the fact that there is little information known about it:

They experience a powerful pull in the direction of the elements, especially water and fire.

They encounter vivid dreams that are eerily similar to real life events.

In many cases, Martian starseeds are motivated by an intense need to contribute significantly to the continued technological and cultural development of the human species.

Andromedan Starseeds

People who are of the Andromendan starseed kind are believed to have originated in the distant galaxy known as Andromeda. Despite the fact that they are only encountered very infrequently on our planet, they are distinguishable thanks to the following characteristics:

They have a kind demeanor and are easy to converse with, according to other people.

They are prone to give off an impression of being childlike, both in their conduct and their looks. Because of this, they come off as pure and distinct from the rest of the population.

They are prone to making extreme choices in order to seek what they believe to be the truth. This may involve giving up a career with a good salary in order to devote oneself entirely to the arts or traveling the world.

Andromedan starseeds place a great value on freedom in all of its forms, including the freedom to choose and the freedom to act.

In terms of their physical appearance, they frequently have a tall and slender build.

They have a strong inclination to engage in creative and spiritual pursuits, like as wiring, composing music, or becoming spiritual instructors.

Starseeds of the Polarian Race

It is believed that Polarian starseeds are creatures from a higher dimension that descend to Earth from the celestial body known as Polaris, sometimes known as the "North Star." Their primary characteristics are as follows:

An intense hunger for knowledge regarding the history of humanity and the method through which it evolved.

Having a natural capacity for empathy with other people.

They have the impression that they are intimately linked to the electromagnetic field of the planet.

They have a hard time understanding why they are here on our world, but they are aware, on some level, that they do have an essential job to complete here.

Venusian Starseeds

The Venusian starseed type has an inextricable connection with Hathor, the ancient Egyptian cow-goddess. Venus is the source of the Venusian starseed type. The following is a list of some of their more notable qualities:

Having an extremely lofty stature.

Having a sexually alluring personality and participating in a plethora of love relationships.

Putting a high priority on their spirituality, to the point that it causes them to lose sight of the duties they have in the material world at times.

experiencing a profound sense of oneness with the world and all things contained within it.

Taking pleasure in the affirmation and care provided by other people.

FAQ

When numerous different sorts of starseeds resonate, what kind of starseed am I?

If you discover that the characteristics of more than one starseed type describe you, you can employ meditation to determine which starseed type best fits you. Simply read through the descriptions, and then, before beginning your meditation, ask yourself the question, "what starseed type am I?" The response is on the way at the appropriate time.

If you are interested in discovering more about starseed awakening and determining whether or not you are a starseed, you may find it helpful to read the list of fifty starseed indicators that I compiled in the past.

What is the most important function that starseeds serve here on Earth?

Starseeds choose to incarnate on Earth so that they might offer some form of wisdom to the people who live there. It's possible that you have a talent for brightening other people's days, or that you feel drawn to work for a humanitarian organization.

Sometimes all it takes to motivate other people is to set an example for them to follow.

How am I supposed to carry out my duties as a starseed?

Your mission on this planet will be unique to you and no one else's since it is determined by both the sort of starseed you are and the exact moment in time that you choose to arrive here. The most important thing to keep in mind is that you have a purpose for being on this planet, and if you listen to your instincts and have faith in who you are, you will be able to fulfill that purpose.

$$$

A free numerology reading is a good approach to learn about your purpose here on Earth and to find out the deeper meaning of your life. Numerology readings are also available online.

Conclusion

Finding out your starseed kind has the potential to alter everything.

As you begin to view yourself from a different angle, the aspects of your life that previously appeared to be holding you back are gradually changed into strengths.

If you are a starseed, the significance of your very existence cannot be overstated.

You have a mission to accomplish while you are on this earth, and I have no doubt that you will succeed in doing so regardless of the challenges you face along the way.

61

Even while it can be fascinating and engaging to think that Starseeds are more advanced than human beings on Earth, the reality is that each and every one of us has the potential to grow at any given time. A person who is a Starseed may or may not have the intention to follow their best self, regardless of whether or not they have the heritage that indicates growth.

It is simple to let oneself become sidetracked by the most charismatic spiritual media personalities or the most up-to-date spiritual belief systems. It is much simpler to feel the need to escape our life and our bodies in order to go beyond the universe and become everything in it.

We don't need to go anyplace else in order to experience true transcendence. We can accomplish it without leaving the comfort of our living rooms.

We are designed to take pleasure in our imaginations and all the fantastical worlds they create. Because of the way that we are built, a single thought may take us to paradise, while an entirely other notion can take us to hell. We as a species are not really steady, if you want to get down to the nitty gritty of it.

Your current "you" is a temporary construct that you continually co-created with your pre-birth guides, as well as the parents and cultures you chose for this life. This is true regardless of whether you are a Starseed, a Muslim, a Lutheran, a Japanese, or an Iranian; whether you are brown or red; whether you are tall or fat; whether you are wonderful, itchy, angry, or hilarious. Nothing of this can be considered definitive.

These are only a few examples of temporary collections of conditions and structures.

Your "you" is only a layer that sits over a magnificent, strong, and alive soul, and you have the capacity to go in whatever path you choose. Your spirit does not consist of lowercase letters;

rather, it always takes the form of a capital YOU. When we allow ourselves to get preoccupied with our limited selves, we run the risk of missing out on opportunities to fulfill a mission and embody the cosmos.

Be extremely cautious about the labels you assign to yourself at all times. Every label is only partially correct, and it only applies to the present time and place. Each of these fleeting versions of oneself comes with its own set of constraints and repercussions. Make an effort to loosen your grip on them a little bit.

Because we answered the invitation to participate in this life, we find ourselves living it.

Live your life as though you are already here, in the present moment. Looking up at the stars might be an enjoyable experience, but going inside is where you'll find the treasure. "Within" will be your permanent abode.

THE END

Printed in Great Britain
by Amazon

87217232R00038